AMERICAN MOSAIC

READING FOR MULTICULTURAL LITERACY

Connections

Linda Gutlohn, Editor

S R A

Macmillan/McGraw-Hill

CONSULTANTS

Dorothy Coakley
Children's Librarian
Bernal Heights Branch, San Francisco Public Library

Juan Carlos Cuéllar
Educational Director/Multicultural Consultant
Mission Cultural Center, San Francisco

Gloria Davis
Executive Director
Access to Higher Education, San Francisco

Terry Halbert
Associate Professor of Legal Studies
Temple University School of Business & Management,
Philadelphia

Doug Haner
Curriculum Resource Teacher
San Francisco Unified School District

Luis J. Kong
Executive Director
California Poets in the Schools

Irene S. Kwok
Bilingual/ESL Resource Specialist
San Francisco Unified School District

J. Cynthia McDermott
Assistant Professor of Education
California State University–Dominguez Hills

Sharon Patacsil
Early Childhood Director
United Indians of All Tribes Foundation, Seattle

Nicky Salan
Bookseller
Cover to Cover Booksellers, San Francisco

PRODUCT DEVELOPMENT

Nanz/Gutlohn, San Francisco

CREDITS

DESIGN AND PRODUCTION: Lucy Nielsen, San Francisco
PERMISSIONS AND PHOTO RESEARCH: Betty Nanz
PROJECT SUPERVISOR: Rick Brownell
MANUFACTURING SUPERVISOR: David Bulicek
COVER MOSAIC DETAIL: Manuel Villamor,
San Francisco General Hospital, Mechanical Building courtyard
COVER PHOTOGRAPH: Ronald J. Hunter

Special acknowledgment is given to Frances Christie, Sahib
Olanrewaju Hassan of *African Roots News Magazine,* Beverly Lozoff,
Charles Pain, Daniel Raskin, Audrey Shabbas, and Beverly Slapin.

ACKNOWLEDGMENTS

For each of the selections listed below, grateful acknowledgment is
made for permission to adapt and/or reprint original or
copyrighted material as follows:

AWAIR: *The Arabs: Activities for the Elementary School Level*, by
Audrey Shabbas, Carol El-Shaieb, and Ahlam An-Nabulsi.
Copyright © 1991 by AWAIR: Arab World and Islamic Resources
and School Services, 2095 Rose Street, Suite 4, Berkeley, CA 94709.

Carolrhoda Books, Inc.: "The Heavy Pants of Mr. Strauss," from
The Spice of America, by June Swanson. Copyright © 1983 by
Carolrhoda Books, Inc., 241 First Avenue North, Minneapolis, MN
55401. Reprinted by permission of the publisher.

The Caxton Printers, Ltd.: "The Winter of the Blue Snow," and
illustrations, from *Paul Bunyan Swings His Axe,* by Dell J.
McCormick. Copyright © 1936, 1957. Reprinted by permission of
The Caxton Printers, Ltd., Caldwell, ID 83605.

Harold Courlander: "How the Hopi Became the People of the
Short Blue Corn," from *Big Falling Snow,* by Albert Yava, edited
and annotated by Harold Courlander. Copyright © 1978 by
Harold Courlander. Crown Publishers, New York, 1978;
University of New Mexico Press, Albuquerque, 1982. Reprinted by
permission of Harold Courlander.

Toni de Gerez: "Ear-of-corn," from *2-Rabbit, 7-Wind: Poems from
Ancient Mexico Retold from Nahuatl Texts,* by Toni de Gerez, The
Viking Press, Inc. Copyright © 1971 by Toni de Gerez. Reprinted
by permission of the author.

Q. R. Hand: "All the Common Sense in the World," retold by Q. R.
Hand. Used by permission of the author.

HarperCollins Publishers: "Chopsticks," adapted from "The Quick
Little Fellows," from *From Hand to Mouth, Or, How We Invented
Knives, Forks, Spoons, and Chopsticks & the Table Manners to Go With
Them,* by James Cross Giblin. Copyright © 1987 by James Cross
Giblin. Reprinted by permission of the publisher.

(Continued on page 80)

INTRODUCTION

MOSAIC ART is made by fitting together small pieces of material such as seeds, stones, or tiles to form a design or picture. Like a mosaic, American society is made up of many different "pieces." Together these pieces, or ethnic groups, form the American mosaic, a society rich in multicultural history and tradition.

One of the problems in a multicultural society is prejudice. Prejudice is disliking or judging a person or group before knowing much about them. Knowledge is one way to overcome prejudice. We hope that the *American Mosaic* series of books will provide you with insight and information to lead you to a better appreciation and understanding of your own unique cultural heritage as well as that of others.

✛ TABLE OF CONTENTS ✛

AMERICAN MOSAIC

✦ **CONNECTIONS**
True and legendary cultural
origins of everyday things,
place names, and celebrations.

✦ **IDENTITY**
Day-to-day life experiences
of members of today's
multicultural, pluralistic
American society.

✦ **SPIRIT**
Feelings, values, and beliefs
of American people as
expressed through their
visual art, music, drama,
dance, and literature.

✦ **VOICES**
Past and present
Americans—both famous
and not so famous—who
have made a difference, a
statement, a contribution,
or have overcome adversity.

THE SECRETS OF
rubber

BY JOHN ROSS

We call the sap of the Hevea tree *rubber* because the inventor of the eraser discovered that it could rub out mistakes. The native peoples who lived in the Amazon rainforest in the center of South America called the sap *caoutchouc* which sounds like a sneeze. But the people of the Amazon probably did not sneeze much because they had their rubber raincoats to keep them dry.

Five hundred years ago, the secret of rubber belonged to the native peoples of the great tropical jungles that stretched from Mexico to the Amazon River of Brazil. These native peoples, whom we call *Indians*, used this amazing sap in their everyday lives.

Ulama is a game that was first played by the Mayans, native people of southern Mexico and Central America. They named this game after the big rubber ball with which they played the sport. The players could hit the ball only with their hips, and when they did, the ulama flew like the sun arching through the sky. To win the game, a player had to hit the ball through stone rings that looked like sideways basketball hoops.

To the Mayans, the game was sacred because they believed playing ulama kept the sun up in the sky. The ulama ball was sacred, too. And so was the tree whose sap they tapped to form the ulama ball.

6

MUNSON-WILLIAMS-PROCTOR INSTITUTE/ MUSEUM OF ART, UTICA, NY

The Mayan ball players could not use their hands to hit the hard rubber ball, only their elbow, wrist, or hip. That is why each player wore a wide belt, a heavy leather apron, and pads on their arms, thighs, and knees. The winners of the game were given jewelry and clothing by the spectators.

sap
the milky liquid latex that flows through a rubber tree

sacred
having to do with religion

rainforest
a tropical forest

When the Spanish came from Europe, they found the Mayans playing the ulama ball game and were amazed. "The ball bounces as if it were alive," they wrote home to their king. Because the Spanish had come for gold and silver, however, they soon lost interest in the rubber balls and the trees from which they were made. A few centuries later, Europeans began to build machines that needed moving parts. It was then that they recalled the magical ways of rubber and how it could be molded into many shapes.

This modern-day Brazilian worker is tapping, or cutting into, a rubber tree the same way the native peoples of the area did long ago. The liquid latex, or natural rubber, slowly runs from the cut into a small container.

The Indian peoples of the rainforest found many uses for the sap of the rubber tree. They used the hardened sap not only to form balls that bounced very high but also to mold bottles, boots, and rubber-soled shoes that always stayed dry. It rains a lot in these jungles, so the Indians put the magic sap on their ponchos to keep them dry. In doing so, they invented the first raincoat long before Charles Macintosh did in Scotland.

8

COURTESY MEXICANA AIRLINES

Now rubber products help us drive cars, fly airplanes, and rocket into space. Rubber keeps us dry, and we still play games with rubber balls. So do the Mayans. Their descendants, the Mixtecs, still play a kind of ulama with a big rubber ball that weighs almost two pounds. They have brought the game and the huge rubber ball to California, where they have migrated to find work.

Meanwhile, back in the Amazon where rubber trees grow, the rainforest is being cut down for its wood and so that cattle can graze there. People like Chico Mendez, a leader of the rubber tree tappers, have tried to stop the destruction. They know that the world needs the rainforests' green plants and trees to make clean air for all of us to breathe.

ACTIVITY

If rubber had not been discovered and used by the Indian people, how would your life be different today? Make a list of all the things you can think of that are made from rubber. Share the list with your class.

This is the Great Ball Court in the ancient Mayan city of Chichén Itzá. Chichén Itzá is located in Yucatan, Mexico. It was built in the fifth century. Two carved stone rings about 25 feet above the ground are located on either side of the court.

poncho

descendant
a person born into a particular group or family

migrate
to move from one place to another

Charles Macintosh
the Scottish chemist who created rainproof coats called *macintoshes*

The Heavy Pants of Mr. Strauss

BY JUNE SWANSON

Levi's® jeans were the creation of a 24-year-old German immigrant named Levi Strauss.

On January 24, 1848, gold was discovered at Sutter's Mill in California. Almost overnight people were coming to California by the thousands, hoping to make a fortune in the new gold fields. In one year San Francisco grew from a small town to a city of 25,000 people. By 1850 the territory had a population of almost 100,000, and in that year California became the thirty-first state.

The new miners needed many things, and usually they had the money to buy whatever they wanted. This abundance of people with money to spend brought a great number of peddlers and merchants to California. One of these peddlers was a man named Levi Strauss.

In 1853 Levi Strauss arrived in California by boat. The trip from the East Coast took him all the way around the southern tip of South America. With him, Levi Strauss brought yards and yards of heavy brown fabric to make tents for the miners and covers for their wagons.

COURTESY LEVI STRAUSS & CO.

Levi Strauss as he looked at 60.

COURTESY LEVI STRAUSS & CO.

The first customers for Levi's pants were California gold miners. These two miners are wearing the heavy pants made by Levi Strauss & Co. in the 1880s.

However, when Strauss arrived in California, he found that the miners needed good, heavy pants much more than they needed tents. None of the pants available were tough enough to stand up against the rocks of the California hills and the hard mining life. So Levi, seeing the possibility for a good business, made his tent fabric into pants instead of tents.

11

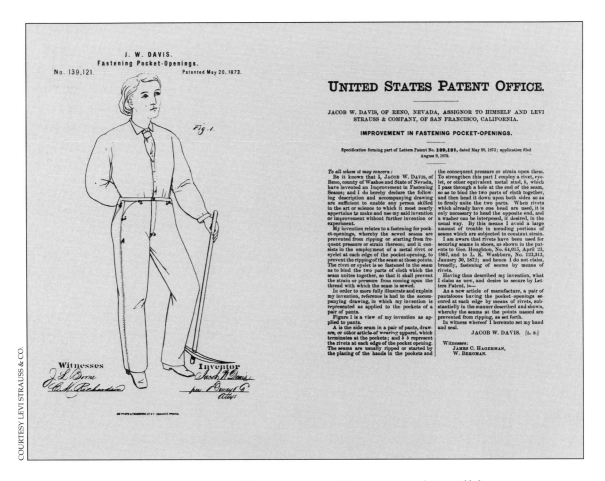

The miners complained that the weight of the gold nuggets caused their pockets to rip. In 1873 Levi Strauss and inventor Jacob Davis received a patent from the government for placing metal rivets, or fasteners, at the corners of the pants pockets to make them stronger.

Strauss's tent fabric was a bit stiff for pants, so in a few years he began to make his pants out of a tough but less stiff material from Nimes, France. The material was called *serge de Nimes*. *Serge* is a kind of material, *de* means "from," and *Nimes* is the name of a city in France. Soon *serge* was dropped from the name, and the material was called *de Nimes*, or "denim."

The miners liked the denim pants so much that Levi couldn't make them fast enough. In fact, his pants were so well made that their basic design hasn't changed in over one hundred years. Somewhere along the way, they came to be called by their maker's first name—Levi.

COURTESY LEVI STRAUSS & CO.

Cowboys and ranch workers, who worked as hard as miners, also wore heavy denim pants. Levi Strauss was the first to color denim dark blue, using indigo dye.

Today the company that Levi Strauss began during the 1850s is still making the same basic straight-legged, button-fly, denim pants that he originally designed for the miners of California. Levi's® have become so popular that they are sold (and copied) all over the world.

From THE SPICE OF AMERICA, by June Swanson.

ACTIVITY

Levi Strauss's inventiveness helped him to find a better use for his heavy fabric. Have you ever discovered a new and better use for something? Share the experience with your class.

Pajamas

W e put on our pj's at night to go to sleep. In India, where pajamas originally came from, men wear loose-fitting, lightweight pants called *pajamas* during the day and at night.

The origin of the English word *pajama* is Hindi, a language of North India. The origin of the Hindi word *pajama* is Persian, a language of the Mogul Empire. Mogul rulers took over India about six hundred years ago.

In India, where it is often extremely hot, men wear their comfortable pajamas at home or at work. Men sometimes wear a *kurta* with their pajamas. A kurta is a long, loose shirt with wide sleeves and no collar. Women wear a long wraparound dress called a *sari*.

The British came to India three hundred years ago and took over the country. They stayed until Mahatma Gandhi won independence for India in 1947. But during their stay, the British had a hard time sleeping at night. Because it was so hot, their long nightgowns and nightshirts were very uncomfortable. Then the British began wearing the loose-fitting, lightweight Indian clothing to sleep in. That is how the Hindi word *pajama* became the English name for the pj tops and bottoms we wear today.

wash day in India

pajama **written in Persian (top)
and Hindi scripts**

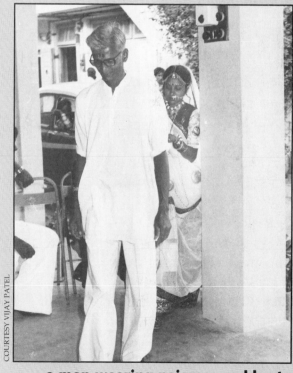

a man wearing pajamas and kurta

Chopsticks

BY JAMES CROSS GIBLIN

The Chinese call their chopsticks *kuai-tse*, meaning "quick little boys." The English word *chopsticks* comes from the expression "chop chop" meaning "do it quick."

No one knows exactly when the Chinese began to use chopsticks. But some say it was greedy people who thought of them first.

According to this story, it happened at the beginning of Chinese written history, around 3000 B.C., when most people cooked their food in tripods. These were metal pots that stood on three squat legs and could be set directly over a fire.

The large pots took an hour or so to cool after the food was cooked, and some people were too greedy to wait. Grabbing a pair of sticks, they poked at the steaming food and lifted out the best pieces for themselves. Others copied them, and within a short time people all over China were eating with chopsticks.

By 400 B.C. people throughout China were using chopsticks. Hand in hand with their adoption came the development of a uniquely Chinese style of cooking. Meat and vegetables were either cut into bite-sized pieces or cooked until they were so tender that they required no cutting. Even when poultry and fish were served whole, the meat was so tender that it could be picked easily off the bones with a pair of chopsticks.

HOW TO USE CHOPSTICKS

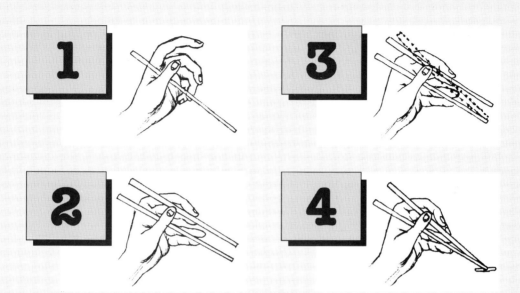

1 Tuck one chopstick under thumb. Rest it on third finger.

2 Hold second chopstick between thumb and forefinger, like a pencil.

3 Use middle finger to move second chopstick up and down.

4 Now you can pick up anything!

Chopsticks have been made from many different materials over the centuries: bamboo, wood, jade, ivory, gold, and silver. Many upper-class families in old China used ivory chopsticks tipped with silver. Since ancient times the Chinese had believed that silver was a protection against poison. If the silver-tipped chopsticks came into contact with food that had been poisoned, they would turn black—or so people said.

bamboo
a plant with a hollow, woody stem

jade
a hard green or white stone

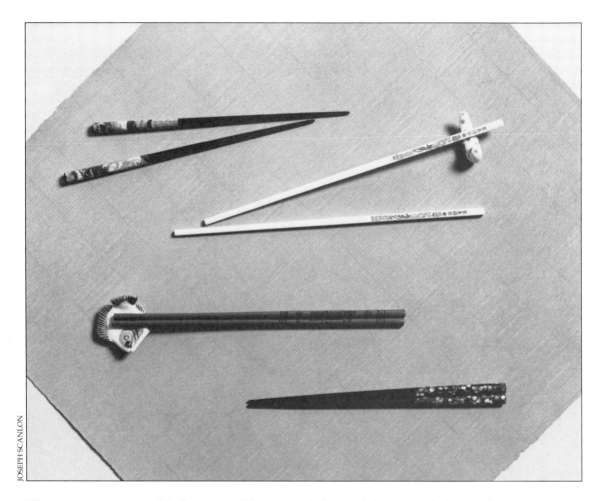

There are two major kinds of chopsticks: Chinese and Japanese. Japanese chopsticks are more pointed at the ends than Chinese chopsticks. Today wood and plastic are the most popular materials used to make chopsticks. Chopsticks are the main eating utensil in China, Japan, Vietnam, and Korea.

The use of chopsticks spread from China to the neighboring countries of Vietnam and Korea. Eventually, like many other Chinese customs, it also reached Japan. This occurred sometime before A.D. 500, and within a short time people throughout the Japanese islands were eating with chopsticks.

The Japanese called their chopsticks *hashi*, meaning "bridge," because the sticks acted as a bridge between bowl and mouth. Japanese chopsticks differed somewhat from the Chinese variety. They had tapered rather than rounded ends and were most often made of lacquered wood instead of bamboo or ivory.

Basically, though, the Japanese handle their chopsticks in the same way the Chinese do. And they've done so for centuries. When a merchant from Italy, Francesco Carletti, visited Japan at the end of the 1500s, he wrote in his journal about the natives' skillful use of chopsticks.

"They are the length of a man's hand and as thick as a quill for writing," wrote Carletti. "With these two sticks, the Japanese are able to fill their mouths with marvelous swiftness and agility. They can pick up any piece of food, no matter how tiny it is, without ever soiling their hands."

Carletti was writing at a time when most Europeans still ate with their fingers. But that would soon change. A new utensil was about to be introduced on dinner tables from Italy to England. This utensil would enable Europeans to eat their food as neatly and cleanly as the Japanese diners Carletti had observed. Eventually it would revolutionize Western table manners.

What was this wonder-working utensil? The common fork.

From FROM HAND TO MOUTH, by James Cross Giblin.

tapered
gradually thinner at one end

lacquered wood
wood with a glossy coating

quill for writing
a pen made from a feather

utensil
a tool

revolutionize
greatly change

superstition
a belief that some action has an effect on a future event

ACTIVITY

It's a Chinese superstition that to drop a chopstick means bad luck. Write a story telling about what happens to someone who accidentally drops a chopstick. Illustrate your story.

All the Common Sense in the World

RETOLD BY Q. R. HAND

There are many folktales about Anansi the spider. These tales are told by the people of West Africa, the Caribbean, and Central America. This story tells how Anansi gave common sense to the world.

They say that the idea came to Anansi just before dawn. First one eye popped open and then the other, as he thought, "I can be rich beyond my dreams. All I have to do is collect all the common sense in the world and keep it for myself. All of it. Every little bit. Then everybody will come to me with their worries and problems. I can charge what I want for my advice because only I will have any to give. I'll be the richest, most powerful spider in the world!"

Anansi, feeling full of energy, went off to gather bits of common sense. He searched and searched all over the world. And every bit he found he stuffed into a huge calabash he had cut from a vine. The calabash became very heavy.

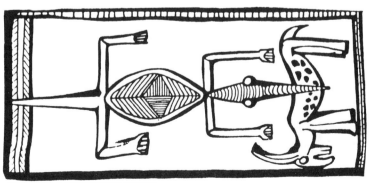

© 1966 PEGGY APPIAH/PANTHEON BOOKS

When Anansi couldn't find any more common sense, he said to himself, "Now I must find a place where my common sense will be safe, where nobody but I can find it." Dragging the loaded calabash behind him, Anansi went to search for the perfect hiding place. He searched through the forest for the tallest tree the sun shines in. The top of that tree would be a good place to hide the calabash.

Sitting on a large root at the base of the tallest tree he could find, Anansi tied the calabash around his neck with a strong rope. With the calabash dangling in front of him, up he went.

common sense
ordinary good judgment that a person learns from experience, not from school or study

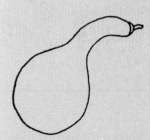

calabash
a large, hard-shelled gourd which grows on a vine

21

Climbing was difficult; the calabash kept getting in Anansi's way. It scraped hard against the tree and felt like sandpaper against his belly. Its weight pulled the rope hard around his neck. The longer he climbed, the heavier the calabash seemed. Remembering his dream of riches and power, Anansi struggled upward. He did not have time or a place to rest.

Anansi was in the middle of his daydream when suddenly he heard a voice burst out laughing from way below, "What a fool you are! If you climb with the calabash hanging behind you, it will not get in your way."

Anansi, who had a very bad temper, glared down through the leaves. He saw a very small boy standing on tiptoe on the large root. He did not like being called a fool by such a small boy with such BIG common sense. How could this be? Hadn't Anansi collected all the common sense in the world?

Anansi forgot for a moment about being rich and powerful. Angrily, he untied the calabash from around his neck. Using all the strength he had left, Anansi smashed the calabash into pieces with one sharp blow. As he watched, the breeze lifted bits of common sense and scattered them all over the world. A little bit went here, and a little bit went there. So nobody got it all. This, they say, is how Anansi made it happen.

© 1966 PEGGY APPIAH/PANTHEON BOOKS

ACTIVITY

Folktales are told all over the world. Like many other folktales, this one teaches a moral, or lesson. What is the lesson? Write another story that teaches the same lesson.

THE HISTORY OF
Sunglasses

BY JOHN ROSS

Today most people wear sunglasses to protect their eyes from the sun. But the Chinese, who invented colored glasses a thousand years ago, used them for a different purpose.

You can tell a lot about what people are thinking just by looking into their eyes. That is one reason why sunglasses were invented. A thousand years ago in China, judges put on dark glasses of smoky-colored quartz to mask their eyes when they were deciding someone's fate. An explorer from Italy saw a judge wearing dark glasses at a trial and took the fashion back to Europe. The rest is history.

Sunglasses, or "shades," come in different shapes and colors of glass. Green glasses are supposed to calm the person who wears them, and red glasses are said to make things look more exciting. When people say a person looks through rose-colored glasses, they mean that the person sees the world in a happy light.

JOSEPH SCANLON

Through the years, sunglasses have come in many different shapes and colors.

quartz
a kind of clear, hard rock

25

Sunglasses keep sensitive eyes from being burned by the ultraviolet rays of the sun. But many people wear them just to be in fashion. Nero, the cruel emperor of Rome, attached a green emerald to his eye when he went to see the gladiators fight at the Colosseum. Hollywood stars wear sunglasses to look glamorous. Jackie Kennedy Onassis, the wife of President Kennedy, made large bug-eyed sunglasses popular. Rock and jazz musicians, like John Lennon and Thelonious Monk, wore shades to look mysterious.

Sunglasses have also been used for military purposes. American soldiers wore old-fashioned sunglasses in the Revolutionary War and the Civil War. In World War II, American pilots wore sunglasses so they could chase enemy planes through the sun's rays. The big, green lenses of the aviator glasses look like mirrors. We call them Ray-Bans®.

Rickey Henderson wore his sunglasses on the day that he stole his 939th base, breaking a major league record.

CHRIS HARDY/SAN FRANCISCO EXAMINER

Just about every American owns a pair of sunglasses. A billion dollars worth of shades are sold each year in the United States. One American who uses sunglasses in his work is baseball star Rickey Henderson. Rickey has stolen more bases than any other baseball player in history. When Rickey gets on base, he puts on his sunglasses. Like the Chinese judges of long ago, Rickey wears dark glasses to hide his eyes, so that no one will know when he is thinking about stealing the next base.

ACTIVITY

The Chinese judges and Rickey Henderson used sunglasses for different reasons. For what other reasons might people want to hide their eyes? Give some examples.

Snow Goggles

The Arctic Circle

When the spring sun melts the ice, Inuit people of the Arctic load up their dog sleds and go off to visit their neighbors. Often, the Inuits' nearest neighbors live hundreds of miles away, so the trips are long. The Inuits never forget to take their snow goggles on these long trips.

Snow goggles, like sunglasses, cut down the amount of light that enters the eye. But instead of being made of colored glass, snow goggles are made of wood or ivory with little slits to see through. In the spring in the Arctic, the bright glare of the sun's rays reflecting off the white snow can cause northern travelers to go blind. Wearing snow goggles prevents snow blindness. When there is a sudden storm, snow goggles also protect the travelers' eyes from blowing snow.

In addition to wood and ivory, snow goggles are sometimes made out of whale bone and walrus hairs. The Inuits carve and paint their snow goggles in many designs and colors. Sometimes, hunters draw animals on their goggles. They believe this helps them to see these animals better when they hunt them.

JOSEPH SCANLON

wooden snow goggles

Just as the heavy fur coat protects him from the cold, this Inuit hunter needs protection for his eyes from the glare and harmful rays of the sun.

ADOBE

BY TONY REVEAUX

Adobe (uh DOH bee) is a building material found in the dry, desert areas of the Middle East, Africa, Spain, Mexico, and the American Southwest. People all over the world have used adobe to build houses, storehouses, markets, forts, and churches.

Adobe is a brick made out of mud, clay, and straw. For thousands of years the people living in the dry, desert areas of the Arab world have used adobe to build their homes. The word for mud brick in Arabic is *ad-dobe*. The Arabs took this word and style of architecture to Spain. In Spain, the Arabic word *ad-dobe* became the Spanish word *adobe*. When the Spanish colonists came to America, they brought the word *adobe* and the Arabs' method of mud-brick architecture with them.

In the Arab world, adobe houses have been built in almost every shape. The walls are usually thick and the ceiling high to keep the house cool in the day and warm at night. The floor may be stone or tile and may be covered with reed mats or rugs. Roofs may be wood, straw, or mud brick.

These mud-brick houses are in northern Syria. They are called beehive houses. *The "hive" acts like an air conditioner, keeping the inside temperatures comfortable even when the outside temperatures get as hot as 140 degrees.*

This mud-brick granary storage system, or ghorfa, is in Tunisia. It is hundreds of years old. A ghorfa can hold an entire village's food supply after a harvest.

31

DON LAINE

Native Americans have lived in Taos Pueblo for 900 years, longer than people have lived in any city in the United States. These clusters of adobe houses were first called **pueblos** *by the Spanish. The word* **pueblo** *comes from the Spanish word for town or village. Each room of a pueblo is a complete house. A house can be added next to or on top of another house as more space is needed.*

The Indian peoples of the Southwest built their houses out of adobe mud long before the arrival of the Spanish. The Pueblo Indians would use a mixture of stones and adobe to build walls in layers, handful by handful. They would let each layer dry in the hot sun until the wall reached the height they wanted.

The Spanish colonists brought to the Southwest the Arab method of making adobe bricks. They added straw to adobe mud and used wooden forms for molding the adobe into brick. The mud was poured into the forms and left to dry in the hot sun. When the bricks were dry, the forms were lifted up, moved to a new spot, and filled again. Then the adobe bricks were stacked to make walls. In many villages the women would coat the outside of the walls with mud plaster.

Adobe dwellings can take many shapes. On the prairies of Utah, where trees were scarce, the settlers used adobe bricks to build houses in the same style as wooden houses.

The Alex Loveridge home was built in Lehi, Utah, in about 1855. There is no plaster on the walls, so you can see the adobe bricks.

The John J. Thomas home was built in Lehi, Utah, in about 1885.

United States

UTAH

NEW MEXICO

This is the Blumenschein Home in Taos, New Mexico. Made of adobe, it was built in 1797. Ernest Blumenschein, an early Taos artist, bought the home in 1919. He lived and worked there for over 40 years. The Blumenschein Home is now a museum.

Adobe bricks are stacked on top of each other to make the walls of an adobe house like the one shown above. Adobe mud is then used to fill the cracks between the bricks. Logs called *vigas* (BEE gahs) are the beams that hold up an adobe roof. The vigas stick out through the walls. The ceiling of an adobe house is made of tree branches called *latillas* (lah TEE yahs) that are laid zigzag between the vigas. Adobe mud is spread over the latillas and smoothed. When it dries, the roof will be hard and strong enough to walk on.

Adobe buildings are cheap, strong, warm in winter, cool in summer, and can be built from local materials. Today the natural adobe style of architecture is popular in hot, dry areas of the United States as well as in other parts of the world.

This modern, ranch-style home in Albuquerque, New Mexico, was designed by Paul McHenry.

Source: THE ARABS: ACTIVITIES FOR THE ELEMENTARY SCHOOL LEVEL, by Audrey Shabbas, Carol El-Shaieb, and Ahlam An-Nabulsi.

ACTIVITY

An Arab Muslim might decorate his or her adobe home with a mural telling the story of a pilgrimage to Makkah. Draw a sketch for a mural that tells about an important event in your life. Write a description of your mural.

Muslim

A Muslim is a person who follows the Islamic religion. Makkah is a Muslim sacred place located in Saudi Arabia. It is a religious duty for all Muslims to make a pilgrimage, or journey, to Makkah, if they are able, sometime during their lifetime.

A Closer Look at KWANZAA

BY DIANE PATRICK

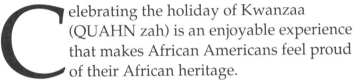

The word *Kwanzaa* comes from the African language of Swahili. It is from a phrase meaning "first fruits." Celebrating the harvest of the first crops, or fruits, is an African tradition.

Celebrating the holiday of Kwanzaa (QUAHN zah) is an enjoyable experience that makes African Americans feel proud of their African heritage.

Kwanzaa can be celebrated in a big way or in a small way. But there are certain activities that are always included.

✹ THE NGUZO SABA (SEVEN PRINCIPLES)

The number seven is very important to the Kwanzaa holiday. There are seven letters in the word *Kwanzaa*. Kwanzaa is also celebrated for seven days, from December 26 to January 1. And there are seven Kwanzaa principles. Every day during Kwanzaa one of them is honored. They are:

1. **umoja** unity
2. **kujichagulia** self-determination
3. **ujima** collective work and responsibility
4. **ujamaa** cooperative economics
5. **nia** purpose
6. **kuumba** creativity
7. **imani** faith

☸ THE KWANZAA SETTING

At home, the family sets a Kwanzaa table. On it, they place the seven Kwanzaa symbols. They are:

1. a **mkeka** (mat), a traditional African item;

2. a basket of **mazao** (crops), which is the symbol of the harvest and the rewards of working together;

3. **muhindi** (corn), one ear to stand for each child in the family;

4. the **kikombe** (unity cup), from which everyone drinks wine or grape juice to honor their ancestors and strengthen unity among themselves;

5. **zawadi** (gifts), to be exchanged on the sixth night. Gifts must always include a book or symbol of black heritage. Children earn their gifts by keeping promises they made in the past year.

6. **kinara** (candleholder), standing for the African ancestors;

7. **mishumaa saba** (seven candles), standing for the seven principles. The center candle is black, three red candles are on the left, and three green candles on the right. Each night, one of the candles is lit, preferably by one of the children. The person lighting it talks about the principle of the day.

Seven Principles

Nguzo Saba
(n-GOO-zoh SAH-bah)
umoja
(oo MO jah)
kujichagulia
(koo gee chah goo
LEE ah)
ujima
(oo GEE mah)
ujamaa
(oo jah MAH)
nia
(NEE ah)
kuumba
(koo UM bah)
imani
(ee MAH nee)

Seven Symbols

mkeka
(m KAY kah)
mazao
(mah ZAH oh)
muhindi
(moo HEEN dee)
kikombe
(kee KOHM bay)
zawadi
(zah WAH dee)
kinara
(kee NAHR ah)
mishumaa saba
(mee-shoo-MAH SAH-bah)

A Kwanzaa table setting showing a straw mat, candleholder and candles, a bowl of fruit and vegetables, and ears of corn.

⚙ KWANZAA GREETINGS

Special Kwanzaa greetings in the Swahili language are used during the seven days of Kwanzaa. The greeting *"Habari gani?"* meaning "What news?" is said every day. The answer is the name of the day's principle such as, *"Umoja."* Then the greeting *"Kwanzaa yenu iwe na heri,"* is said, meaning "May y'all's (your) Kwanzaa be with happiness."

✪ THE KARAMU (FEAST)

The **karamu** takes place on December 31, the sixth night of Kwanzaa. It involves several families, or the whole community. Everyone helps prepare the food. Before and during the feast, everyone takes part in a program of entertainment and discussion.

At the end of the feast, the **tamshi la tutaonana** (farewell statement) is made. The speaker leads the community in the **harambee** (call to unity) and reminds everyone to work together.

✪ CHILDREN AND KWANZAA

Children are important to Kwanzaa. They can help with the Kwanzaa setting, make Kwanzaa cards and decorations, and help prepare the food. But they are especially important because they inherit African culture and are responsible for preserving it and helping it grow and develop. Through Kwanzaa, they learn a lot about their African heritage and help to make sure it continues.

Kwanzaa yenu iwe na heri!

From HARAMBEE, November-December 1990.

ACTIVITY

Dr. Maulana Karenga, an African-American professor, created Kwanzaa in 1966. Create a holiday to celebrate pride in yourself. Design an invitation to a special holiday event. Include a list of your holiday's principles with the invitation.

Habari gani?
(hah-BAH-ree GAH-nee)

Kwanzaa yenu iwe na heri.
(QUAHN-zah YAY-noo EE-way nah HEH-ree)

karamu
(kah RAH moo)

tamshi la tutaonana
(TAHM-shee lah too-tah-ohn-AH-nah)

harambee
(ha RAHM bay)

moon festival

BY IRENE S. KWOK

Most Chinese in America observe the Moon Festival. This harvest festival, like Thanksgiving, is a traditional time for families to get together. The Moon Festival is also known as the Mid-Autumn Festival.

The Moon Festival is a time when Chinese families get together for a family reunion to give thanks for the foods they grew and harvested during the year. It is also a time when the Chinese celebrate the way they gained their freedom from the Mongols in the fourteenth century.

The Moon Festival is celebrated on the fifteenth day of the eighth month of the lunar calendar, or in the month of September or October according to the Gregorian calendar. This is the time of the Harvest Moon, the brightest and fullest moon of the year.

The day of the Moon Festival as shown on a Chinese lunar calendar.

Moon cakes are a symbol of family unity. According to tradition, a cake is shared among family members.

During the month before the Moon Festival, stores display moon cakes and beautiful lanterns in their windows. Moon cakes are made of white flour. They are formed and baked in the shape of the moon. Most are the size of a donut and are filled with coconut, lotus seeds, or nuts. The top of each moon cake is decorated with the Chinese character for *autumn*. People buy moon cakes for their families, or to send to friends and relatives as gifts.

Homemade lanterns are also part of the Moon Festival celebration. The brightly colored paper lanterns are symbols of hope for a bright and prosperous future. There are many different lantern designs, but most are made in the shape of fruits to represent the harvest.

harvest
gathering a crop when it is ripe

lunar calendar
The lunar calendar is based on the cycles of the moon. It has 354 to 360 days per year.

Gregorian calendar
This Western calendar is based on the cycles of the sun. It has $364\frac{1}{4}$ days per year.

lantern

41

On the evening of the Moon Festival, family members get together for a delicious dinner. Special desserts are set out in sight of the moon. Fruits such as apples, oranges, pears, bananas, pomelos, and persimmons are beautifully displayed along with peanuts, boiled taro root, and moon cakes.

When the full moon appears, a moonlight ceremony begins, which includes the burning of incense. Candles are placed in the lanterns, and the family members carry their lanterns outside. There they wish each other well and eat dessert together. Later the children play games and carry their lanterns as they visit friends in the neighborhood. When the candles in the lanterns burn out, the festival is over.

the moon cake story

In the fourteenth century, China was invaded by the Mongols. The Chinese people decided to revolt against their cruel rulers. The day of the revolt was secretly set for the fifteenth day of the eighth month, the same date as the Mid-Autumn Festival. The leaders of the revolt chose this holiday because everybody would be home with their families.

Since there were many Mongol spies in the community, the date of the revolt had to be kept a secret. The Chinese needed a plan to deliver the message to revolt without the Mongols knowing. A clever man, Lau Pak Wan, came up with an idea. He suggested that the message be written on little paper squares and put inside the moon cakes which were to be made for the celebration of the Mid-Autumn Festival.

Then, as was the custom, the Chinese gave the cakes to all their friends, neighbors, and relatives. The Mongol spies did not notice anything suspicious.

When the moon cakes were cut open, the Chinese found the secret message about the revolt. On the fifteenth day of the eighth month, the Chinese rose up against their Mongol rulers and drove them out of China. From that time on, when people see moon cakes during the Moon Festival celebration, they feel a special pride. They remember when the cakes were used to help win freedom.

pomelo
a large, yellow citrus fruit

persimmon
an orange-red fruit

taro root
a brown root about the size of a large potato

the moon lady, sheung ngao

The moon is very special to the Chinese. They believe that it is poetic and mysterious, bringing good luck and a bright future. Its roundness is a symbol of family unity, something very important in Chinese culture. For these reasons, many Chinese folktales and stories have been written about the moon and have been passed down through the generations.

Many, many years ago in China there was a powerful king who was evil. This king had a beautiful wife whose name was Sheung Ngao.

The king heard about a magic medicine that would keep him young forever. He ordered many people to search for the magic medicine, but no one could find it.

Then the king ordered a few hundred people to sail in large boats far out into the sea. He said, "Do not come back until you have found the magic medicine that will keep me young." The people finally found the magic medicine that would keep a person young and brought it to the evil king.

Sheung Ngao, the king's wife, knew that the king was not a good person. She did not want him to live forever. So, to help the people, Sheung Ngao stole the magic medicine from the king and swallowed it herself.

As soon as she had taken the medicine, Sheung Ngao floated up to the brightest spot in the heavens—the moon. It was a safe and peaceful place and she knew she would be happy there.

The people were very grateful that Sheung Ngao had saved them from the wicked king. Every year on the fifteenth day of the eighth month they remember her with the Moon Festival celebration. Sheung Ngao lives on the moon to this very day.

Sheung Ngao

random thoughts at mid-autumn festival

The night is cool as I lie stiff on the steel bunk.

Before the window the moon lady shines on me.

Bored, I get up and stand beneath the cold window.

Sadly, I count the time that's elapsed.

It is already mid-autumn.

We should all honor and enjoy her.

But I have not prepared even the most trifling gift

and I feel embarrassed.

From ISLAND: POETRY AND HISTORY OF CHINESE IMMIGRANTS ON ANGEL ISLAND 1910-1940, by Him Mark Lai, Genny Lim, and Judy Yung.

From 1910 to 1940, Angel Island in San Francisco Bay served as an immigration station for Chinese coming to America. The Chinese were forced to stay on Angel Island for questioning. Their stay could last from weeks to months, or even years. This poem, shown in Chinese on page 47, is one of the many that were written on the walls of the barracks on Angel Island.

中秋偶感
夜涼僵臥鐵床中，
窗前月姊透照儂。
悶來起立寒窗下，
愁把時計已秋中。
吾儕也應同敬賞，
菲儀無備亦羞容。

elapsed
gone or passed by

trifling
unimportant or
worthless

immigration
moving to a country
in which one was
not born

barracks
buildings where
workers or soldiers
live

ACTIVITY

The Moon Festival is one of many harvest festivals celebrated around the world. Compare the Moon Festival to other harvest festivals such as Thanksgiving. How are these festivals alike, and how are they different?

POW-WOW!

BY BEVERLY SLAPIN AND JOHNELLE SANCHEZ

A pow-wow is a large social gathering for Indian people. Pow-wows go on throughout the year and can take place once a year, once a month, or once a week. Some things are always the same about a pow-wow—lots of singing, lots of dancing, and lots of great food!

Cool breezes break through the heat. The air is filled with the heavy fragrance of sage smoke and the aroma of strong coffee and cooking fry-bread and Indian tacos—those are the smells of the pow-wow.

Drums, flutes, bells, jingle dresses, laughter—those are the sounds of the pow-wow.

Pickups and canvas tipis and feathers and beads and silver and turquoise and shell and coral and bone, in every color imaginable—those are the sights of the pow-wow.

Children are everywhere—running freely, screaming with laughter. No one worries that anyone will get lost, here, today. Everybody takes care of everybody's children. Old ladies with bandanas folded over their foreheads to shade them from the sun sit on folding chairs and cool themselves with rolled-up paper fans.

BEVERLY SLAPIN

✤ TRADITIONAL POW-WOW FOOD ✤

Indian fry-bread

Fry-bread is a relatively new tradition of the Indian people. In the 1800s the United States government forced the Indian peoples onto reservations. On the reservations the government gave the people unhealthy, surplus food called *commodities.* The people combined two of these commodities, white flour and lard, to make fry-bread.

Indian tacos

Indian tacos are made of rice, beans, shredded meat, lettuce, tomatoes, and cheese piled high on a piece of fry-bread, and covered with salsa. Yum!

---

tipi

A tipi is the traditional home of Indian peoples from the Plains. The word *tipi* comes from the Dakota words *ti* and *pi. Ti* means "to dwell," and *pi* means "used for." Traditional tipis are made of buffalo skins, and modern tipis are usually made of canvas.

49

HULLEAH TSINHNAHJINNIE

Around the pickups and cars, everyone is
helping everyone get dressed. Grandmothers, aunts,
and mothers dress the children—fixing jewelry,
adjusting roaches, tying feathers, braiding hair.
Children are so excited they can hardly hold still.

Four little girls meet. They are about four years
old. Three are dressed in fancy-dance regalia; the
other in a t-shirt and jeans.

"How come you're all dressed like Indians?"

"We *are* Indians!"

"Me, too!"

Giggling, they run off together to find an adult
who will buy them a taco.

The sun filters into the arbor as the drummers sit down around the drum. Everything is a circle.

During the week, the dancers are math teachers, plumbers, chiropractors, carpenters, cab drivers, students. The weekend is a time for socializing and dancing and eating, and coming together as many Nations, one people.

A drummer picks up a drumstick and begins. The drummers start their slow, steady beat. Someone asks a blessing. Dancing starts slowly at first. Sometimes the children fool around, but now they are very serious because they know the eyes of the Elders are on them.

roaches
headpieces made out of porcupine fur, worn by men and boys

regalia
traditional clothing worn by Native people for dancing or special ceremonies

arbor
a shelter made of branches

BEVERLY SLAPIN

BEVERLY SLAPIN

Women's traditional dances, men's traditional dances, fancy dances, intertribal dances. There may be contest dancing. People in jeans and sneakers dance beside people in full regalia. Some dancers start as soon as they can walk. Even babies dance, in the arms of their parents or grandparents.

It's late afternoon; the sun comes shining through the dust. Some people keep dancing as long as they can find someone to drum for them. Nobody gets much sleep at night on a pow-wow ground.

BEVERLY SLAPIN

Nobody ever wants to leave when it's over. Everybody sort of mills around, finding one or two last things that they have to say to somebody. It will be dark before most people leave. A few tipis are left up. A few trailers remain for the people who will stay overnight and leave in the morning. It's quiet now. The pow-wow is over.

fancy dances
beautiful outfits and very difficult dance steps, generally for a contest

intertribal dances
people from different tribal backgrounds dance together

ACTIVITY

A pow-wow is a traditional American Indian celebration. Find out about a tradition that a parent, grandparent, or Elder in your community enjoyed as a child. Then tell about or draw a picture of it.

Cornrows

BY CAMILLE YARBROUGH

Cornrows are a special braid design once worn only by African queens. Every design has a name and means something in the rich African tradition.

Great-Grammaw was fixin Mama's hair in cornrows. That's what Great-Grammaw calls those braids. She said the braids got that name because our old folks down south planted rows of corn in the fields. And the rows in the cornfields looked like the rows of braids that they fixed in their hair. Mama's hair was lookin pretty.

So I said, "Fix my hair in braids, Great-Grammaw."

And MeToo said, "Fix my hair in braids, Great-Grammaw."

Then I said, "What's the name of your style, Ma?" . . .

And she said:

I delight in tellin you, my child—
yes, you please me when you ask it—
it's a hair style that's called *suku*.
in Yoruba, it means "basket." . . .

Folk singer Miriam Makeba is a native of South Africa.

UPI/BETTMAN

Then Mama told me to bring the stool and come sit down so she could fix my hair. Mama and Great-Grammaw always sing a little bit before they tell their stories. They say that's so they can get in the mood.

When I heard Mama start singin real quick, I sat down on the stool in front of her and said, "Mama, tell me a story about cornrowed hair."

And real quick, MeToo looked up at Great-Grammaw and said, "Great-Grammaw, tell me a story about cornrowed hair, too." And Mama started singin:

Uuuum, I'm tellin a story about cornrowed hair. . . .

An Great-Grammaw said:

Um, um, um, um, um.
I'm tellin a story about cornrowed hair. . . .

Then Great-Grammaw put MeToo down on his little chair so she could get at his head, and she said:

Child, come an sit by my knee,
an I will tell you about your family tree.
An I will dress you
as a prince should be,
an the right name will come
to both you an me.
An I will braid your hair,
an I will braid your hair. . . .

TRADITIONAL YORUBA CORNROW STYLES

SUKU
(shoo KOO) * basket

IPAKO ELEDE
(ee-pah-CAHW eh-LEH-deh)
back of the head of a pig

KOROBA
(koh roh BAH) * bucket

KOLESE
(koh LEH seh) * without legs

Yoruba
(YOUR oo bah)
the language of West African people living in Nigeria

family tree
a chart showing all your past and present relatives and how they are related

55

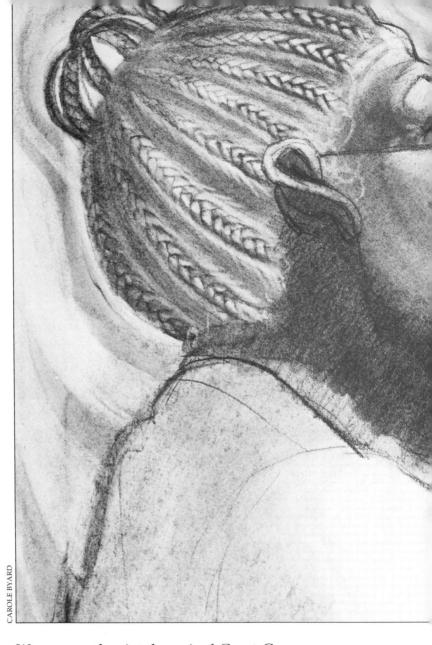

CAROLE BYARD

We were real quiet then. And Great-Grammaw started tellin the story:

"There is a spirit that lives inside of you. It keeps on growin. It never dies. Sometimes, when you're afraid, it trembles. An sometimes, when you're hurt an ready to give up, it barely flickers. But it keeps growin. It never dies. Now a long, long time ago, in a land called Africa, our ancient people worked

ancient
very old

praise
thanks

symbol
something that stands
for something else

through that spirit. To give life meanin. An to give
praise. An through their spirit gave form to symbols
of courage, an honor, an wisdom, an love, an
strength. Symbols which live forever. Just to give
praise."

Then Mama said:

Some symbols took form in . . . braided hair.

57

MeToo asked Mama, "Who was wearin the
braided hair?"

"Ooh, lots of people," Mama said. "Everywhere
you looked. Almost everyone that you would see.
People from Egypt to Swaziland. From Senegal to
Somali."

You could tell the clan, the village,
by the style of hair they wore. . . .
Then the Yoruba people
were wearin thirty braids and more. . . .
You would know the princess, queen, and bride
by number of the braid. . . .
You would know the gods they worshiped
by the pattern that they made.

"Then a terrible thing happened."
I said, "What, Mama?"

The clan,
the village,
the priest,
the bride,
the royalty,
all were packed into the slaver ships
and brought across the sea . . .
where they trembled on the auction block
and on the chain-gang line . . .
where they flickered on the pyre
and while hangin from the pine. . . .
And the style that once was praise
then was changed to one of shame.
Then the meanings were forgotten
and forgotten was the name. . . .

MeToo asked Great-Grammaw, "Did the
spirit die?"

And Great-Grammaw said:

No such thing!
If you're quiet
you can still hear the royal rhythms,
still feel the spirit in the air.
Look around an you will see the old, old symbol
that we now call cornrowed hair. . . .

From CORNROWS, by Camille Yarbrough.

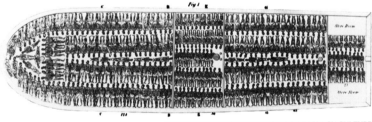

SCHOMBURG CENTER FOR RESEARCH IN BLACK CULTURE

diagram of a slave ship

ACTIVITY

Mama wore her hair in cornrows as a symbol of her African spirit. Describe the way you wear your hair and explain your reasons for wearing it that way. Does your hairstyle have a name?

Egypt, Swaziland, Senegal, Somali
countries in Africa

clan
family

slaver ships
slave ships that carried captured Africans from West Africa across the Atlantic Ocean to the New World

auction block
a place where African slaves were sold to the highest bidder

chain gang
Slaves were chained together so they couldn't run away.

Our Mother Corn

BY UNITED INDIANS OF ALL TRIBES FOUNDATION

Corn, also called *maize*, is a plant that has been part of Native American cultures for thousands of years. Today, many Hopi, Papago, Seneca, Navajo, and other Native American peoples raise and use corn in the same way their ancestors did.

The Pawnee and Hopi tribes call the tall, life-giving plant "Mother Corn." The Seneca tribe says that corn and woman are one—the mother—for both give life and care for the people. Many other Native American cultures owe their lives to corn. Long ago it was their main food.

Corn was a central focus of life for the tribes that depended on it. Special prayers, chants, songs, dances, and ceremonies honored and gave thanks for corn. Today many farmers still sing as they work. The Navajos' Farm Songs are poems and prayers that celebrate the beauty of planting and bring good thoughts to the farmer.

> I wish to plant.
>
> In the middle of the wide field
>
> I wish to plant.
>
> White corn, I wish to plant.
>
> With soft goods and hard goods,
>
> I wish to plant.
>
> The good and everlasting corn
>
> I wish to plant.

OUR MOTHER CORN

THE ORIGIN OF CORN

T housands of years ago, most likely in a tropical area of Mexico, a wild, cornlike grass was planted and cared for by Indian people. Corn, or *Zea mays*, developed over time, probably through a process of selecting and then cultivating the seeds from the tallest and best quality grasses.

The cultivated corn was different from its wild relative. The seeds or kernels would not sprout without the help of people or animals. The kernels had to be taken off the ear and then covered with soil.

Because corn was easy to grow and could be stored for a long time, it became an important source of food. It also became a valuable trade item and quickly passed to many tribes all over the United States. Corn was responsible for saving the lives of many early European settlers who might otherwise have starved.

Mandan, Choctaw, and other Indian tribes developed and grew a wide variety of corn. Some corn was eaten fresh from the cob. Other corn was ground into meal or flour. Popcorn was grown and popped by Pueblo, Zuni, and other Indian people thousands of years before the first movie theaters tempted audiences with it.

When we picture corn in our minds, we think of yellow or maybe white corn. But tribes like the Mandans and the Hurons grew corn in many other solid colors. The colors ranged from orange to maroon to purple and even to black. Speckled corn and calico corn were also grown. Calico corn had several colors on one cob.

ROGER FERNANDES/DAYBREAK STAR PRESS

Zea mays
the scientific name for corn

cultivate
to prepare and use land for growing crops

1 Choctaw
2 Hopi
3 Huron
4 Mandan
5 Navajo
6 Papago
7 Pawnee
8 Pueblo
9 Zuni

The exact origin of corn still remains a mystery. But there can be no doubt that it has played a major role in the development of the Americas. From its beginnings in some warm, wet region of the New World, growing corn has spread to the deserts of the Southwest, the cold northeastern United States, and to many other places around the world.

From OUR MOTHER CORN, by United Indians of All Tribes Foundation, Daybreak Star Press.

HOW THE HOPI BECAME THE PEOPLE OF THE SHORT BLUE CORN

Humans emerged into this land from a world beneath the earth. When the people came out, the mockingbird arranged them according to tribes, the tribes they were going to be. He said to one group, "Sit over there. You will be Comanches." To another, "Sit over there. You will be Hopis." Another, "Sit over there. You will be Bahanas, or white people." After that, the mockingbird set out

ROGER FERNANDES/DAYBREAK STAR PRESS

the corn. He put out different kinds of ears, all the varieties of corn that we know. He told all these tribes to take whichever ears they wanted, and he told them what each ear meant. He said, "Now, this yellow corn will bring prosperity and enjoyment, but life will be short for whoever chooses it." And when he came to the short blue ear, he said, "This one, the blue corn, means a life of hardship and hard work, but the people who choose it will have peaceful times and live to a ripe old age." He described all the different ears, and the leaders of the tribes sat looking at the corn, trying to make up their minds.

Then one big tall fellow, a Navajo, said, "All right. You people can't decide." So he reached out and grabbed the long yellow corn that meant a short life but much enjoyment. The others said, "Ayih! He's always grabbing!" Then everybody began to grab. The Supais took the yellow speckled corn. The Comanches took the red corn. The Utes took the flint corn. Every tribe got its corn, but the leader of the Hopis sat there without taking anything until only one ear was left, the short blue corn. He picked up the short blue ear and said, "Well, this ear is mine. It means we will have to work hard to live, but we will have long, full lives."

From BIG FALLING SNOW, by Albert Yava. Edited and annotated by Harold Courlander.

prosperity
success and wealth in life

hardship
something that causes suffering or difficulty

flint corn
corn with very hard seeds; name comes from a hard rock called "flint"

1 Comanche

2 Hopi

3 Navajo

4 Supai

5 Ute

ACTIVITY

The mockingbird put out different ears of corn for the leaders of the tribes to choose. Which ear of corn would you have chosen— the long yellow corn or the short blue corn? Explain why.

Ear-of-corn

AN ANCIENT AZTEC POEM

The most sacred of all Aztec foods was corn. The ancient Aztec people of Mexico believed they owed their knowledge of growing corn to Quetzalcoatl (kayt zahl KO atl), god of agriculture. According to legend, Quetzalcoatl is believed to have discovered grains of corn in the crack of a rock.

Aztec poems were recorded in picture books called *codices*. Codices were made from sheets of maguey paper or from deerskin. The sheets were folded so that they could be opened like a screen. They were usually about sixteen feet long and about seven inches wide.

The words of this poem were probably first sung or chanted. They formed part of a sacred ritual dance and ceremony.

Ear-of-corn

you are a copper bell

you are a fruit pit

you are a sea shell

white   white

you are crystal

white   white

you are a green stone

you are a bracelet

you are precious

you are our flesh

you are our bones

Quetzalcoatl

From 2-RABBIT, 7-WIND: POEMS FROM ANCIENT MEXICO RETOLD
FROM NAHUATL TEXTS, by Toni de Gerez.

✴ American ✴ Place Names

BY ROGER A. HAMMER

Readers can be writers, too! These authors were asked to tell about their city, state, or school and how it got its name. Their stories were published in *"My Own Book!"* There are 54 stories in *"My Own Book!"*—one from each state, the District of Columbia, Puerto Rico, Guam, and the Virgin Islands.

✴ NORTH HAWAII AND HONOLULU, HAWAII
The Mystery of the Red Water
by Maile Bean
Age 10

There are many places in the Hawaiian Islands that are named "Waimea." Each Waimea is named for its unusual reddish-brown water that flows into the sea when it rains. Each Waimea also has its own special story of why that particular area is named Waimea or reddish water.

I would like to tell you the story about the Waimea where I live. My Waimea is located on the "Big Island" of Hawaii, 60 miles northwest of Hilo and 45 miles north of Kona. Miles and miles of grassland cover my beautiful Waimea as well as many groves of eucalyptus trees that act as wind breakers.

Hawaii Statehood 1959-1984
USA 20c

In 1629, King Charles I of England granted his attorney general, Sir Robert Heath, a large parcel of land. It was located between the 31st and 36th parallels and from the Atlantic to the Pacific. It was called *Carolana*. Carolana is from the Latin word *Carolus*, which means Charles, in honor of the King who had given the land.

In England in 1642, civil war erupted between King Charles's followers and the Puritans, who were led by General Oliver Cromwell. After the Puritans won, they cut off King Charles I's head! Sir Heath was among the thousands forced to flee England. Two years later in 1660, Cromwell, who had been ruling England, died.

Charles II, the dead king's son, returned from exile and decided to reward eight men who had helped him regain his right to the throne. He added part of Florida to the grant and changed the name to *Carolina*. The word *South* was added in 1730 when North and South Carolina became separate colonies.

As you can see, the naming of South Carolina involved many years and several interesting events.

From "MY OWN BOOK!" by Roger A. Hammer.

ACTIVITY

There is often more than one explanation for, or story about, the origin of a place name. Find out how your city, town, or state got its name. Write about it.

script
Railroad workers were paid in "script." Script was a form of money issued by the railroad to be used at the company store, saloon, etc. As the railroad was built, the place where the script was issued and spent (the "script town") moved with the work and the workers.

parallel
an imaginary line that circles the earth and is used to mark off latitude

Puritan
a person who was a member of a group of Protestants in England during the 1500s and 1600s

exile
to send a person away from his or her country or home as a punishment

AN ISLAND CALLED

California

Baja California

In 1510 Garcí Ordóñez de Montalvo of Spain wrote *The Adventures of Esplandián*. This popular novel of the time tells about the adventures of Esplandián, the son of Amadís. Among the places Esplandián visits is one "on the right hand of the Indies, . . . an island called California, very close to . . . Paradise, populated by black women, without a man among them, whose lifestyle is like that of the Amazons . . . . their island was the strongest in the world, with its steep cliffs and rocky shores. Their weapons were all of gold, and so was the harness of the wild beasts which they tamed and rode. For in the whole island there was no metal but gold." This island kingdom overflowing with gold, gems, and pearls was ruled by a beautiful black warrior queen named Calafia.

When an early Spanish explorer landed in what is now Baja California, he mistakenly believed that he had come upon Montalvo's fictional island paradise called California. By 1542, about ten years later, navigators were using the name *California* to describe the Baja peninsula.

Queen Calafia

by Aswad Arrif

Queen Calafia black as ebony

and as beautiful as the dawn;

long braids with gold dangling

from them;

jewelry that sparkles

in the sun;

power greater than anything I

have ever seen.

Leader of the Amazons;

wealth, beauty and great power,

Calafia Oh, Calafia.

From DANCING ON THE BRINK OF THE WORLD, by California Poets in the Schools in association with Oakland Unified School District.

The Winter of the Blue Snow

BY DELL J. McCORMICK

Paul Bunyan was a super lumberjack of the North Woods. No job was ever too hard for Paul and Babe the Blue Ox to handle. This tall tale tells about how "The Land of Sky Blue Water" got its name.

One night in the North Woods the men were seated around a campfire. They were telling of their adventures in other camps. Someone asked Paul to tell them of his earlier adventures.

"Tell us about the Winter of the Blue Snow," cried Tiny Tim.

"Well," said Paul, "I was logging with my father back in the Maine woods. That was the winter I found Babe the Blue Ox. Only he was a little calf then not much larger than Tiny Tim. Old-timers sometimes speak of it as the year of the two winters. When summer came, it got cold again, and in the fall it turned colder. For two solid years the snow covered the ground so deep that only the tops of the tallest trees showed through the snow.

"The snow was blue in color and over two hundred feet deep in places. The Great Lakes froze solid to the very bottom and would never have thawed out if loggers hadn't cut the ice up into small blocks and set them out in the sun to melt. When spring finally came, they had to get a complete new set of fish for the lakes.

"The camp was buried under the snow, and the men rode up to the surface in elevators. Each man had sixteen blankets so that he would be warm at night. Shot Gunderson, who was head sawyer, can tell you how cold it was. He slept under forty-two blankets, and one morning he got lost and couldn't find his way out. It was three days before we could find him, and by that time he had almost starved to death.

"It was so cold that when Hot Biscuit Slim set the coffee out to cool it froze so fast the ice was hot. The men had to eat breakfast with their mittens on, and sometimes the hot biscuits were frozen solid before they could take a bite.

Paul Bunyan and Babe the Blue Ox

Paul Bunyan towered above the trees of the forest and combed his beard with a young fir tree. With his giant ox, Babe, he roamed the forests from Maine to California. His footprints were so large they filled with water and became known as lakes. When he shouted to his men, whole forests were blown down with the force of his mighty voice.

sawyer
someone who saws
wood

"The bunkhouses where we slept were so cold that the words froze as soon as the men spoke. The frozen words were thrown in a pile behind the stove, and the men would have to wait until the words thawed out before they knew what was being said. When the men sang, the music froze and the following spring the woods were full of music as odd bits of song gradually thawed out.

"Very few trees were cut that winter as we had to make holes in the snow and lower the men down to the trees. Then we would pull the trees out of the holes with long ropes.

"The men all let their beards grow long as a protection against the cold. Some of the beards were so long that they got in the way, and the men were always stumbling over them. So we made a new rule in the camp. Anyone with a beard over six feet long had to keep the end of it tucked in his boots. In the spring the beards were so thick the men had to shave them off with axes.

"When Christmas came that year the men were homesick for some good old-fashioned white snow. 'It doesn't seem like Christmas,' they cried, 'with all this bright blue snow on the ground.'

"So I decided to put on snowshoes and travel west until I could find some white snow. Well, sir, I climbed over mountains and across plains right out to the Pacific Ocean, which was frozen solid. The ice seemed fairly thick, so I kept on going. And do you

know I had to travel clear to China before I could find any white snow! But the men were certainly happy when I brought them back some white snow for Christmas!

"We had a lot of trouble with frost-biters that winter. They were little animals about three inches long that lived in the snow. They bit the men on the feet as they walked along. Even now, you hear of people being frostbitten, but that winter it was much more dangerous.

"The blue snow finally melted in the spring and filled many lakes in the woods. To this day, many of the beautiful lakes in the mountains are still colored blue from the Winter of the Blue Snow. The Indians called the country 'The Land of the Sky Blue Water.'"

From PAUL BUNYAN SWINGS HIS AX, by Dell J. McCormick.

ACTIVITY

A tall tale usually has a hero, hardships, humor, and lots of exaggeration. Write a tall tale about a modern super hero. Make sure to tell where your hero lives and his or her occupation.

snowshoes
flat, webbed frames attached to boots for walking over deep snow without sinking into it

frostbite
harm to some part of the body caused by freezing

"The Land of Sky Blue Water"
The state of Minnesota, in the North Woods, is often called "The Land of Sky Blue Water." The closest English meaning of the Dakota Indian words *minne* and *sota* is probably "cloudy water." Politicians changed the Indian meaning to "sky-blue water" because they thought it sounded better! *Clouds* are in the *sky*, and the *sky* can be *blue!*

(Acknowledgments, continued from page 2)

Just Us Books, Inc.: Adapted from "A Closer Look at Kwanzaa,"
by Diane Patrick from *Harambee*, November-December 1990.
Copyright © 1990 by Just Us Books, 301 Main Street, Suite 22-24,
Orange, NJ 07050. Reprinted by permission of the publisher.

Irene S. Kwok: "Moon Festival," by Irene S. Kwok. Used by
permission of the author.

Munson-Williams-Proctor Institute: Figure of a Ballplayer, c. 550-
950, orange pottery, 5 5/8" high x 4 3/4" long, artist unknown
(Mayan). Photo used by permission of Munson-Williams-Proctor
Institute, Museum of Art, Utica, NY.

Oakland Unified School District: "Queen Calafia," by Aswad Arrif
from *Dancing on the Brink of the World*, The California Poetry
Curriculum 1984-1985. Copyright © 1985 by Oakland Unified
School District. Reprinted by permission of Oakland Unified
School District, Oakland, CA, and California Poets in the Schools,
870 Market Street, Suite 657, San Francisco, CA 94102.

Pantheon Books: Illustration from *Ananse the Spider: Tales from an
Anshanti Village*, by Peggy Appiah. Copyright © 1966 by Peggy
Appiah. Reprinted by permission of Pantheon Books, a division of
Random House, Inc.

The Place in the Woods: "The Land That Looked Like Velvet," by
Mary Loraas, "The Mystery of the Red Water," by Maile Bean, and
"The King Who Lost His Head," by Kristen Lee Tabbutt, adapted
from *"My Own Book!"* by Roger A. Hammer. Copyright © 1987
The Place in the Woods, 3900 Glenwood Avenue, Golden Valley,
MN 55422-5302. Reprinted by permission of the publisher.

The Putnam Publishing Group: Excerpted from *Cornrows*, text ©
1979 by Camille Yarbrough, illustration © 1979 by Carole Byard.
Reprinted by permission of Coward-McCann, Inc.

Tony Reveaux: "Adobe," by Tony Reveaux. Used by permission of
the author.

John Ross: "The History of Sunglasses," "The Secrets of Rubber,"
and "Snow Goggles," by John Ross. Used by permission of the
author.

Beverly Slapin and Johnelle Sanchez: "Pow-Wow," by Beverly
Slapin and Johnelle Sanchez. Used by permission of the authors.

United Indians of All Tribes Foundation: "Our Mother Corn," and
illustrations, adapted from *Our Mother Corn*, developed by Sherry
Mathers and edited by Bill Brescia. Copyright © 1981 by Daybreak
Star Press, P. O. Box 99100, Seattle, WA 98199. Published by
United Indians of All Tribes Foundation, a public nonprofit
corporation. Reprinted by permission.

University of Washington Press: "Random Thoughts at Mid-
Autumn Festival," in Chinese and English, from *Island: Poetry and
History of Chinese Immigrants on Angel Island, 1910-1940*, by Him
Mark Lai, Genny Lim, and Judy Yung. Copyright © 1991 by
University of Washington Press. Reprinted by permission of
University of Washington Press.

Every effort has been made to trace the ownership of all
copyrighted materials in this book and to obtain permission for
their use.